Crypto Chuckles

Charles R. Baumstark

ISBN-13: 978-1542958653

Welcome to Crypto Chuckles!

By way of a short biography, I am a graduate of Fordham University in New York. Subsequently, I served in the U.S. Navy for three and a half years, during which time I was a crypto security officer. I am currently a retired community banker.

I enjoy doing puzzles, crosswords, Sudokus, and cryptograms etc. Most of the cryptograms I've seen are derived from famous quotes or famous humorous sayings or jokes by well known personalities.

I decided to create some original "quips", which I call "chuckles" and encrypt them, thus Crypto Chuckles.

I hope they bring a smile to your face and a few laughs to share with your family and friends.

Crypto security back in the navy,
Crypto Chuckles in retirement.

Good luck and enjoy.

Chuck Baumstark

CONTENTS

1

OD G DKXRIKGIMP QUUPRVGJ IEKMQ EOR EGIFEMI OJIU G QUUPFEUYYOJL VGFEOJM, QUXNP BUX RGB EM EGP GJ GZM IU LKOJP?

Clue:
L = G

2

I YIPCUP IBO KEJ LEYU OUFEOUO AV KIMU NICX FKVRJ YVP OEBBUP. IYAUP MEULEBH XVAK AKU CINU IBO YUCINU NICXJ, AKUQ OUFEOUO AKU YUCINU NVVSUO CVPU AUBOUP. AV LKEFK AKU CINU UGFNIECUO "XUAAUP ULU AKIB CU".

Clue:
E = I

3

C EUIWK RUILAD ZW AUBD MUUO C NCAO UW CW UAH FUCXHNCAO ZW C XUPCWMZR URDCW XDQUXM. CM MVD DWH UT MVD NCAO MVDE HZQRUBDXDH MVCM MVDE FUMV VCH NUUH RVZLQ ZW MVDZX TDDM, FIM OZQQDH CWH VIKKDH CWENCE. AUBD ZQ C PCWE QLAZWMDXDH MVZWK.

Clue:
R = C

4

L SZUND UB TPOSCKUZF JCU JPZP TUX OTQOXPH XU L BZOPTHF JPHHOTS, MZLFCPH XCP MPZPIUTA LTAJLA. JUNVH XCPA KP MLVVPH "ILZZA DUD-OTF"?

Clue:
V = L

5

P XPR RPXJH WPJDPL QCTRH P RJO SJLKPF AJP WPFFJH "ATD" (AJP TDURE DPEJ). OSJR SJ BUDUAJH P QLUJRH SJ OPD DTLZLUDJH ASPA SUD QLUJRH DJLBJH SUX ASJ DPXJ AJP. WPJDPL JGWFPUXJH "VCT ACC KLJO ATD".

Clue:
Z = P

6

I XIK BTOOUDUE ODQX TKFQKLDQJJIVJU VJIEEUD YDQVJUXB, BTFS LSIL SU FQTJEK'L EIKFU IL I YIDLP JUBL SU MUL SRB YIKLB. SU MIB RKLDQETFUE LQ EUYUKEB. SU MQDU LSUX QKU EIP LQ I YIDLP IKE RL MQDCUE. MQTJE LSIL VU SRB RK EUYUKEB EIKFU EIP?

Clue:
R = I

7

FR H RXEKZHP BFZKQMSZ LHFEMO UFO NKUFQPK VKPPSD FEOMKHB SR MUK MZHBFMFSEHP WPHQC, DSXPB MUHM WK H UKHZOK SR H BFRRKZKEM QSPSZ?

Clue:
U = H

8

ZC R GKIC MRDUIIW RPW MILNIW R XIRB UKRU PSESWA GSDBW WZMGILP FKRU ZU FRM XRWI SC. FSDBW UKRU EI RP DPZWIPUZCZIW CLAZPT SEVIGU?

Clue:
L = R

9

UCBBX KIQVIGIH VB TICGIB CBH TIQQ, KJA FCR PMBGVBPIH TI FCR NMVBN AM TIQQ CBH FCBAIH AM KI CR PQMRI CR WMRRVKQI. TI QIOA C DIEJIRA VB TVR FVQQ AM "KJDX UCBBX QMF".

Clue:
P = C

10

CTGQY M XMDOKHZMDL CNT MLLKDYO LT LNK NMHY TA NKMHWDP RK EMQQKY '" M ZMQKL TA YKMA"?

Clue:
X = M

11

NZ IFR ILUUKJ'R DLV MKUUNL YEG E DHDDA, CKHUG NV WL "E ILUUKJ MKUUNL WEWA"?

Clue:
L = E

12

CO G RGH MWXRWWO OGXCNOL CX HWGIIV JNWLOX BGXXWH RFN RGL HCSFX. RFGX BGXXWHL CL RFN CL IWDX.

Clue:
S = G

13

FK I ZXGA AXGKP WXRZ VXGAKIEDKV, FZ MXG UFAPFD VOD ZFATV OXRD FK VOD ZFATV AXGKP, MXG WDV I UMD FK VOD KDYV VLX AXGKPT. FT VOIV I" UMD UMD UFAPFD"?

Clue:
F = I

14

ASDH UKDQYAUE LUEAUX ESQDJJDJ EFKD ASDDED EF ISYW ISUI WFGFJZ YW ISD QDEIUCQUWI AFCXJ DPDW IUEID YI. EF, ISD LUIQFWE UXX ESFCIDJ " KUND UKDQYAUE VQUID UVUYW"!

Clue:
C = U

15

RO S AJKVIMNO QDSOVSVRJO, RG VIM JLOMNA AMV KQ S TMDD VJLMN VJ SDMNV VIMP LIMO S AVJNP SQQNJSBIMA, LJKDU VISV TM S “ZJOZ LRVI VIM LROU”?

Clue:
A = S

16

HD E UEDREVA UKFPVR, HU ED PSL, E GHDP EDC ED KET GIR KD E VSEG VRHBT BKLPCA FKIRHDP, OKISC RJER QP BESSPC "RJP RFPP VRKKYPV"?

Clue:
P = E

17

L DLT ZLY USNF XM IOY FSWUSB US TKCKB FBOTQ WSVVKK. IK WOUKF L UKWITOWLNOUM LTF YULBUKF FBOTQOTE NLUUK, KHWNLODOTE “XKUUKB NLUUK UILT TKCKB”.

Clue:
N = L

18

W XPICHDLRZF SWITDFM AWL CMPERTRUFK VMPI CDWXROS WOJ IPMF AWSFL WU UEF XWLROP. LP EF FODRLUFK W VMRFOK UP CDWXF UEF TFUL VPM ERI. APHDK UEWU TF XPOLRKFMFK “WRKROS WOK WTFUUROS”?

Clue:
A = W

19

Z XCHEV HB BCKRLNF FKA ZCHELN ZSS NZG NHKLX LHAIKLX, AIKLMKLX LHAIKLX ZLN FZGKLX LHAIKLX. HLR NZG Z WZL FAZLNF EV HL Z PIZKC ZLN VCHPSZKWF "K ZW AIR SRZFA KLARCRFARN VRCFHL HB ZSS HB EF". QHESN IR JR PHLFKNRCRN AIR PIZKCWZL HB AIR JHCRN?

Clue:
V = P

20

LE J XYLHLQZ QSYNOMT JTR J S.Q. BORLD UOYEMYBOR QSYNOYV MT JT LTKSYOR QMWRLOY'Q OWXMA, AMSWR HZJH XO DJWWOR "J KMLTH MUOYJHLMT"?

Clue:
K = J

21

EO AYENVE CEMMR, E GEVAYAN TPMM GER RPO FL OQ EMPVO EFOJQVYOYPR YC RQUPTQIB CPMM QDPV OJP CEMMR. YC OJP TPMM GPAO QCC TB EKKYIPAO, GQFMI OJEO TP E “CEMMR EMEVU”?

Clue:
P = E

22

H VTLFC CUSO YMK LN H YKHFJ KT YMOO RLNY TX RLYKHSJ. H NTOURMDHF HYWMJ ZMS UX YZM ZHJ H NMSDUK. QZMF YZM HFYQMSMJ FT, ZM YZLK ZMS JTQF. QTLOJ KZHK IM "RLYKHSJ'Y OHYK YKHFJ"?

Clue:
Z = H

23

RSN ZNYRUNE TBT EH JFIS RLYKNUBVX RSYR RSNBL IUHRSNE ZNIYJN EHBUNT KNLM PFBIDUM, SHGNKNL, RSNM ZNIYJN NWONLRE YR UYFVTNLBVX GBRS Y OHOFUYL TNRNLXNVR YUJHER TYBUM. BE RSYR GSM RSNM YLN IYUUNT “RSN CYZ CHFL”?

Clue:
M = Y

24

B IBS SBIOT QBVN ZOM ER B UOC ZJMO UAOKO BSD IOICOK VLEYT ZUBR MAOJK IOKVASTJZO UJMA BSD LMAOK IOICOK SL IBMMOK MAO SBMEKO LK HBYEO. ULEYT AO CO VBYYOT "B QBVN LP BYY MKBTOZ"?

Clue:
C = B

25

CP D MBKVHQ INB FJDLQHQX FNQ ZHBWQ NDX D MNCHX WBJO DF FNQ OBJFN VBHQ DOX BOQ WBJO DF FNQ UBKFN VBHQ, IBKHX FNQ MNCHXJQO WQ MBOUCXQJQX "WC-VBHDJ"?

Clue:
X = D

26

CY QY NUBQVMB LMKICWY WR VPM RQFWNI KQGM XMVZMMY Q KQXXCV QYB Q VWKVWCIM VPM KQXXCV QGVNQSSA ZCYI, XNV WYSA XA Q “PQKM”.

Clue:
X = B

27

LSRZYMMRS UQUY XSYQUYN Q ELM MKMUYO UGQU QDTQKM UQBYM KRJ UR UGY TSRAE LDQXY. GY XQDDYN PU UGY UQUY MKMUYO QAN MRDN PU JMPAE UGY MDREQA "GY TGR GQM Q UQUYM PM DRMU".

Clue:
X = C

28

WN ZH HNG RJHLS LSLXPLF Z EPZFWMD ER PUZP HR DZPPLS JULSL ARMS ELZP JZE GRXZPLF, ARM UZF Z TLSNLXP MHRKEPSMXPLF BWLJ RN PUL IZDL, XRMGF PUL XRHPLEP KL XZGGLF Z "NZH-PR-ELL NRRPKZGG IZDL"?

Clue:
G = L

29

JC X FBXMNXG ZXI X UVBYS BD KJGJNXVI KAHJFM TAVA ZAJCU JCMNVYFNAH XM NB LBT NB FXVA DBV MTJKKAVM MYDDAVJCU DVBK XC XGUXA ZGBBK. FBYGH NLJM ZA FXGGAH "ZXI-MJFE NVXJCJCU"?

Clue:
D = F

30

K RWEGOEOSROVE KLZOVQL FOV NHOQREV ES LGORP EQK LWGORM EFQ CKHH, VKXORM EFKE EFOV DSWHL TQ EFQ TQVE NHOYKEQ CSG EQK. KHH EFQ NHOQREV NSYJHKORQL EFKE EFQX YOVVQL EFQOG EQK. DKV EFQ RWEGOEOSROVE WVORM "CKHH-EQK HSMON"?

Clue:
P = K

31

U WUH HUWTO VZO PFUHRTH KFTUQTO U VTTF WZS QCUQ EUD DN ZSMA QCUQ GQ EUD PFGSCQTHGHS QN TLTFANHT ECN DUE GQ. VZO KUMMTO GQ CGD “PFUHRTH-DQTGH”. CGD PFGTHOD TBKMUGWTO QCUQ QCTA QCNZSCQ VZO EGDTF QCUH QCUQ.

Clue:
Z = U

32

I FWGK TDG I HKQYV OEISHDZKO EHTKFLEDH EHUDYKO I HKKOYK EHMKFLEDH QPEFP IYZD GKZWYLKO EH I ZLIGLYEHS HKWGDYDSEF GKIFLEDH. FDWYO LPEZ NK FIYYKO "ZLEFCKG ZPDFC"?

Clue:
E = I

33

ZC HBNYALDW'H UBLDW DQKYA YIP ZH WP QPWIYA MDNDVQY PC KADWHCPALZWI ZWKP KUY MDNYS MABHDSYA, RPBQS UY VY AZSZMBQYS DWS MDQQYS "MQDAF MDW'K"?

Clue:
S = D

34

AO LWW USC SDXECE DK L XLKVS NCXC OCF USC SCLWUSACEU CBRAKC ODDF LGLAWLMWC, NDRWF USLU MC VDKEAFCXCF L “EULMWC FACU”?

Clue:
W = L

35

GH BALVRB BIJN OIBBFLRZ SFJVDF BGOAUGFLXFB VLB OIHHFUFB HUAD BFDFLXGV QAIRB TF XTFL SFJADF "BVHHZ BIJN"?

Clue:
O = S

36

TK PYL YTVYRZ UDWYTUPTSGPLH VGIHLK DC L-HLK, TC GHGN AGU GXRL PD YGSB TKPD LJL'U WITJGPL T-WYDKL, ADMRH ZDM UGZ YL PDDB G "XZPL DC PYL CDIXTHHLK GWWRL"?

Clue:
V = G

37

UM NQW DOIO GVVWYOE QM XIULLUPJ YQSORQEN YQ XKGX XKON YXWSRBOE GPE UPHWIOE XKO HQUPX UP XKO SUEEBO QM XKOUI BOJ, DQWBE XKGX RO VQPYUEOIOE G “MOBB-QP-CPOO”?

Clue:
J = G

38

EX FIP XUSS NSCWPFNSOO UISGVELXCIEVC, FIP OPSHDP IPOK S HLOZ FLDMXSGPXF. LX FIP OSCF ILOP, S VOSBPM IEF S HLOZ NSOO FISF ZOPJ EX FIP KEMPUFELX LZ SXLFIPM HLOZPM SXK BPOOPK "ZLMP". ULDOK FISF NP USOOPK "FIP ZEXSO ZLMP"?

Clue:
C = S

39

MEYIN O BEIVKD EHHVKDZ MAE MEYIN KESGQOSQIX GSDOW EHH NYZVST IYSKA AEYZ QE QOWD O SOB LD KOIIDN “OS YSNDZKERDZ KEB”?

Clue:
E = O

40

Y AWXLMH ZHUH NBOBJBGT JDH YMYSW ZDHG JDHQ TWJ BGJW YG YUTXSHGJ, JDH ZBCH CHMM YGI RUWFH JDH SBIIMH VWBGJ BG DHU MHT YGI JDHQ TWJ IBNWUAHI. JDH DXORYGI AYMMO DBO SWGJDMQ LYQSHGJO JW DBO HP-ZBCH "YMYSW-FGHH".

Clue:
Q = Y

41

NGKP FHKI RKZ MGD SOKEHPV VMOU RCLP KP LYYKPD VMOU ZCMD SGPQDGYLF CHZ OLV. QMGOF DCKD AL QKOOLF "K CMOL HP NGKP"?

Clue:
K = A

42

UC DRB MFYD RUMB UI DRB QFYDBNY HUMI DUGNCFQBCD OC HBUNHOF, DRB MBFTBNY JFMM SFY JMUSC UGD UI JUGCTY JZ F YDNUCH JNBBAB FCT RB MUYD DRB DUGNCFQBCD. RB JMFQBT ROY MUYY UC “FGHGYDF SOCT”.

Clue:
I = F

43

D RHXNC XY YHVPZUA BFX OPK YXH ODZM MPDHA VZ D ACPEVDI ANVKP DK D YDZEM FXKPI UVAEXZKVZNPU KFP RDKFPHVZR UNP KX XIU DRP DZU VIIZPAA. DA XZP YHVPZU ADVU, CDHKVZR VA ANEF "ANVKP AXHHXB".

Clue:
U = D

44

XW OW CWZXF TOFLDPPR O YPROW RXUFOISWZV TDCULSJ LSD FSSFL YXFL NZCS HDPR O FXW FCTS FLOF ZPPISJ ZXIS FPPFLKOUFS. ULS YOU CWOTZS FP SOF HPD USESDOZ JOVU. ULPCZJ ULS TS PW O "NZCS-FXW HDSS JXSF"?

Clue:
P = O

45

RJ CDH VNWQ GJ PGLWC GURKH GEHWHM NW GJJRSH RW N SGPEHCRWF VNWQ'I UHWMRWF NOHN, AGLUM CDNC VH SGWIRMHOHM "HYCHWMRWF NW GURKH VONWSD"?

Clue:
N = A

46

DO B IWBSJT ABRWBOJ JVW PSQRWZ VBQ JY XVYYZW JVW CDOOWM BFYOR JVMWW LDOBUDZJZ; FBMT, JWMMT BOQ XVWMMT. DL JVWT XVYZW JVW UBJJWM, CYSUQ JVBJ IW XYOZDQWMWQ "XVWMMT ADXNDOR"?

Clue:
I = B

47

KE K XSURUJXV ZJUEOLKT RKUET, JAXEVKL MW XMBVZMLT RMRRJAC MSE MW K YKUCV DKFV, K IMDKYJXE XEMML MA EMR KAL XKAC OKRRT ZJUEOLKT. DMSYL EOKE ZV DMAXJLVUVL "EOV J-XJAC MA EOV DKFV"?

Clue:
F = K

48

I MQIWJZ DETJQGJITJ FIG PEHXTC JPIJ GPQ FEWKO MQ DBEFTQO JPQ FXTTQB. MWJ GPQ DINQ XT GQDETO. ET JPQ FIZ ELL JPQ GJICQ GPQ JBXHHQO ITO DBIDUQO I JEEJP. GPQ CEJ PQB "DBEFT" ITZFIZ.

Clue:
X = I

49

CE S QCGVXM QWXFGA FRKMOSORV ONWFRI QWFMGSFGPA GW SMMRMM CGM QXMGWYRVM MSGCMESQGCWF KCGN GNRCV OVWIXQG. KWXPI AWX MSA GNSG KSM S QCGVXM QWXFGA "QNVWFCQ-QSPP"?

Clue:
M = S

50

D ODV IM NKY VDOY UH JYABE EBHHYF XJDMYW NKY XDFN UH DV DVPYJ BV D GKFBENODE XDPYDVN. WSFBVP NKY XYFHUFODVGY, KY NFBXXYW DVW HYJJ. GUSJW KY IY GDJJYW "JYA EBHHYF NKY HDJJYV DVPYJ"?

Clue:
W = D

51

TH QAYV ZCTQC QWR UYAFQWX RMBMSYFMR Q UCMQA KOQK GOMW QFFSTMR KY KOM MXMV QSSMBTQKMR QSAYVK QSS MXM QTSAMWKV. VOYESR KOMX AQCIMK KOM FCYREUK EWRMC KOM VSYPQW "HQAYEV QAYV ZCTQC'V MXMV UCMQA"?

Clue:
B = V

52

D GJEBXO KIPEXAOL DIL ZOXXOL DA ODGU JAUOW JSOW PJCO AWKSKDX CDAAOW, MEA AUOI XDAOW GJEXLI'A WOCOCMOW JW RKQEWO JEA YUZ AUOZ YOWO DWQEKIQ KI AUO RKWPA BXDGO. AJ AUOC KA MOGDCO "D GWJPP-YJWLP BENNXO".

Clue:
L = D

53

DA D AJVDH, AKS TSGSFMS DAALJFSR EJLAS D WLSI WJLBHDVIVFP KVM BHVSFA'M VFFLBSFBS. AKS ZXTPS JSWHVST, DHAKLXPK RLX BDF JKRIS, KS KDM AL TL AVIS, AKSJS VM FL CDVH, KS VM PLVFP AL ZDVH. ELXHT AKVM CS "WLSAVB ZXMAVBS"?

Clue:
T = D

54

C ECO BCS CO CL DY XQW C DSY LYAACG AYDDY DNJTZD UYG YOZ LYAACG. SFZO FZ SZOD DY DFZ BDYGZ YO BQOLCW DY XQW DFZ DNJTZD, FZ LNBJYIZGZL DFZ BCAZ ZOLZL BCDQGLCW. SYQAL WYQ BCW FZ SCB "C LCW ACDZ COL C LYAACG BFYGD"?

Clue:
C = A

55

LYOFVHWB ODVN BTDHC LDE DC DRBQV QIF CDOQE WBDVN BTDHC TLF DRTDKW RFFNQE FC BLQ EDVN, WBDVN WHEQ FP RHPQ. ADWQE FC ODVN'W WBKRQ FP TVHBHCI, BLQ UVHBHUW EYVHCI LHW RHPQ TQVQ SVQBBK UQVBDHC BLDB "CQXQV BLQ BTDHC WLDRR OQQB".

Clue:
E = D

56

SOWE V UVIB VKLWI V RVE OTS OQK JTUA SVK JTQEJ, OW NWGUQWI "UQLW XUQEZ WVKZSTTI". KOW NWKGTEIWI "QZ RVLWK BTDN IVB?" ET, OW KVQI "QZ'K ZOW JTTI, ZOW HVI VEI ZOW DJUB".

Clue:
Q = I

57

CM QTJ XHAPCPHQYG FVAACAI MJF QOY OCIOYGQ JMMCXY CA QOY NHAP XJLKYQYP CA H XJAQYGQ QJ GYY TOJ XJVNP FYLJSY H TJFL MFJL H MCGOOJJD QOY UVCXDYGQ, TJVNP QOHQ EY XJAGCPYFYP H KFYGCPYAQCHN PY-EHCQ?

Clue:
O = H

58

U LYOVNQ EQK YJ UJ YJ-NMJQ CUKMJT ZQFWMLQ. KPQS ZPUFQC XULQDYYG UJC KBMKKQF, DOK JQWQF EQK MJ VQFZYJ, UJC BQFQ EUFFMQC MJ U WMFKOUN LQFQEYJS LUNNQC BQC YJ KPQ BQD. LYONC SYO ZUS KPQS "Q-NYVQC"?

Clue:
O = U

59

W KNTGENWERI JCOJURY KWNQRN SWG DFFUOYB EF GRR OK COG CRYG SFTDI KOYWDDV DWV RBBG. ECRV SRNR LWNNRY KFN QFYECG. SCODR CR SWG SWEJCOYB, GTIIRYDV ECRV IRDOPRNRI. JFTDI COG FLGRNPWEOFY LR JWDDRI “RBB-GOBCEOYB”?

Clue:
S = W

60

RDI XKNRKWL QU RDI LIE SQOT GRKRIL WGCKLV UIOOS OIXQALRIV RQ RDI NKGGILMIOG KCC QU RDI HKLS GROKLMI DKNNILWLMG RDKR QXXAOOIV VAOWLM DWG ZQSKMIG WL RDI DKOJQO. EQACV RDKR JI XQLGWVIOIV “UIOOS-RKCIG”?

Clue:
T = K

61

Y XTMQC CZJV JPKPZAPE Y KSYJU DJYKPVPI GJTU YQ YEUZJPJ ZQ SZCS BKSTTV YQE YQTISPJ KSYJU DJYKPI GJTU Y KTVVPCP DPYM. MVIZUYIPVX, BSP UYJJZPE SPJ NJZQKP KSYJUZQC. RTMVE XTM BYX BSP VPE Y "KSYJUPE VZGP"?

Clue:
X = Y

62

WV ETWEEBP BSWZEBC WK MKNWBKE APBBNB, THXQC EIB JBZZMAB ZBKE BSNQMWJWKA EIB CWZNHFBPR HV EIB VHPJXQM VHP EIB MPBM HV M NWPNQB LB NMQQBC M “ETBBER-DW”?

Clue:
J = M

63

LK XJB HVFR MY XJB PMTVK UMZMRRBET, V IMTVK JVH XJB YLPRX XPVKRSBKHBP MCBPVXLMK VKH QBUVTB V SZVHLVXMP. HEPLKS V QVXXZB, XJB MCCMKBKX RVLH FME YLSJX ZLWB V YBTVZB. XJB PBRCMKRB IVR "QBBK-JBP".

Clue:
P = R

64

QLFJ PLF XGJ YFLRJE PLF TAGPF RJ G YGZFYGAA VGXF MFGKPZ GJVMRAB PN PLF YGPPFM'Z KNJZPGJP NYIFKPRNJZ PN LRZ KGAAZ. QNHAE BNH KGAA PLGP "HXT-RMF"?

Clue:
V = G

65

AKCUB LZ G RUCWDCZY BPNBQCJCLZ CZ JKB GDLL WLOZJGCZE CZ CZQCG, LZB WLOZJGCZBBX GEMBQ JKB LJKBX, "ALOUQ JKB KCYKBEJ NLCZJ CZ JKCE XGZYB DB RGUUBQ NBGM-GDLL"?

Clue:
Y = G

66

QRFV E DJTXUF QRJ REC PFFV BEYYHFC GHGIW WFEYN REC IRFHY QFCCHVO YHVON NIJUFV, IRF RTNPEVC PJTORI VFQ YHVON GJY JVF XFVVW FEDR. QRFV RHN QHGF CHNDJLFYFC IRF DJNI NRF FMDUEHBFC “WJT EYF IQJ-DFVI-E-BFVIEU”.

Clue:
F = E

67

L IYXXEZ ILYXIBLT IMYP DMMPI AM STISIQXOAKTD OSIAMBXJI ACLA YLAXJ ASJTXP MSA AM WX MWTMGKMSI LTP PKIDSIAKTD QJMPSOAI. CX BLPX L YMA MR BMTXZ KT ACX QJMOXII. VMSYP ACLA WX OMTIKPXJXP "DJMII" QJMRKA"?

Clue:
Y = L

68

MSO KGMCWLB WI G QOCPGL COBMGACGLM KCGUBOF MSO WXLOC IWC MSO JAGZUMR WI MSO IWWF WL MSO POLA, EAM BAQQOBMOF SO FW PWCO GFTOCMUBULQ MW ULVCOGBO MSO TWZAPO. SO VWPKZUOF XUMS MSO BZWQGL "WAC ECGMB GCO MSO XACBM".

Clue:
Q = G

69

H RDISU UOQY SHZVC ZHQR, AFD AHN HJQHOC DJ GFV CHQE, AHN UOBVS H NZHYY OYYIZOSHGVC CVBOWV GD WHYZ FVQ JVHQN HG SOUFG. ZOUFG RDI NHR “ZHQR FHC H YOGGYV YHZM”?

Clue:
F = H

70

M LKBVXRMT DVUU MTX RTHWIVX QRO UVF JQRLQ LMWOVX QRB AK JMUE JRAQ M URBZ. QV IVLKWTAVX AQV RTLRXVTA AK QRO MWXRVTLV RT AQV DKIB KD M QWBKIKWO OAKIS. BRFQA AQMA NV LKTORXVIVX M "UMBV HKEV"?

Clue:
B = M

71

DXJTC THUPCJ VYB KWFKECQ EX Y LYPPXVCCW TXBEHZC NYUEJ. LXVCFCU, LC QKQ WXE PKOC VCYUKWR GYOC XHEGKEB, BX LC VCWE YB LKZBCPG. K RHCBB “DXJTC VKPP DC DXJTC”.

Clue:
J = Y

72

FDTK ERJJC ALXXPBRK, NDT OLEXPVDTJ IQ R ARGIJ VCKUPYRNTU KTFVOROTJ DPN R ERU VDIN IQQ NDT QPJVN NTT PK R XIYRX BIXQ NILJKRATKN, FILXU DT URJT VRC "UI P BTN R ALXXPBRK?"

Clue:
J = R

73

M FULH KLFZKLK GJ NMAL M NMGFU JH NMIYLS YJMRLO. NWG UL WOLK OJ YZGGYL HYJWI ZD GUL ILFZBL, GUL NILMK GWIDLK JWG GJ NL LEGILQLYS OQMYY. GUL BMGIJDO JH GUL ILOGMWIMDG OFILMQLK “GULOL MIL NMILYS YJMRLO”.

Clue:
Q = M

74

VO QJUQMJA IVPYKYVO OVIQU PQMMA LVE VUIYDDQU DH V SHIQ GHM DSQ VPQU. SHLQBQM SQ KHODYOXQU DH WQMGHMI GHM DSQ HDSQM WVDYQODE. DSQA MQGQMMQU DH SYE WQMGHMIVOKQ VE “PQMMA-VD—DMYKRE”.

Clue:
B = V

75

RJHHW KDPN VJN J RJN FOXNOXUW FD SXFOHLOHO ZSFV OGOHWRDNW OPIO'I RMISXOII. VSI LHSOXNI UHOJFON JXN EHOIOXFON FD VSQ J IEOUSJP FHDEVW FVOW UJPPON "J KDPN QONNPO".

Clue:
F = T

76

SMD DMMLJ, V RJLP LMDVKSTX CJKSGJDVK WVF AJJK DVLLTJO SJK STDJF VKO TF JKCVCJO SM VKMSWJL GMRJGP GVOP BWM BTGG AJXMDJ WTF JGJRJKSW ALTOJ. WTF ELTJKOF LJEJL SM WTD VF SWJ “DMMLJ SWJ DVLLTJL”.

Clue:
R = V

77

BQ GXKBNG G WPKM ZX DQSO DKGUPM GNKZOO CWP EGOC RFGBQO. CWPQ G OLGFF DKZSR IKZVP GTGA GQM XZKLPM CWPBK ZTQ WPKM. TZSFM CWBO IP NZQOBMPKPM "IKPGVBQD DQSO"?

Clue:
D = G

78

R CIXQG XJ RIMYRNXWXCOLDL, BYOWN NPGWXIOAC DYN HQACWNL XJ RJIOMR TOLMXUNINT DYN INFROAL XJ RA NPDOAMD DIOEN DYRD YRT NVQOAN JNRDQINL. BXQWT DYRD EN DNIFNT R “YXILN IRMN”?

Clue:
I = R

79

FBWG BLJYEJE JLYQO JM SBYWJ JCQ IYNQWQEE MV B TQBPJYVPI ZYLI TG JCQ WBFQ MV OQQ, B WYKNWBFQ VML EBWOG, TPJ JM WM BHBYI. VYWBIIG EMFQTMOG XBE EPKKQEEVPI. JCQ MJCQL BLJYEJE SMWOQLQO "CMX'O CQ OM OQQ"?

Clue:
T = B

80

NJ F DKHSG HD UORRW, ND F DRLFKR, VOH OFT F SHKT, UJRRMRT. VHAKT NX IR WEHWRE DHE XOR LFKR UORRW XH UFP "YHT IKRUU RVR"?

Clue:
D = F

81

D FPVTS VY LBRFIJVPRLF EITPEIBA EVLQTEWBQ D SVGG WV QBWBPKRLB XIREI VY WIBRP PBGRFRVTA GBDQBPA XDA EVLARQBPBQ WIB JBAW. XVTGQ WIB XRLLBP JB EVLARQBPBQ “WIB SPRKB KRLRAWBP”?

Clue:
Q = D

82

RK F VRBM TDKAJC'L MFZ, F ECRNW RP FODM AJK-WDK FMORVFAJL LJA NW FK FBBJZ RK F PCRYJK WRKM. VRNBM ASFA IJ VFBBJM "F IRTB RP VSDBBZ"?

Clue:
P = F

83

KNYJ AXDL PT OXEXBWXL KZXTKA SYSKN KNX DLBA NDO KP NDRG WDEV KP JNPLX D WDGGYJKYE BYJJYGX KNDK BYJSYLXO. YK ZYGG WX SPLXCXL VTPZT DJ KNX “BYJJYGX-KPZXO ENLYJKBDJ”.

Clue:
O = D

84

TMU VNAAC ORE LNC QHMALUH TMLR VNAAC ENCOKHUUE MR OFIMCA UGUHJALNRK, ORE OC O HUCSFA ALUJ VUHU WMRCAORAFJ BNKLANRK UOWL MALUH. VMSFE ALOA QU WMRCNEUHUE O “QOAAFU MB ALU VNAAC”?

Clue:
M = O

85

B OANBV MZKHLBXTW SLT CBXS FSTNX AV XBCT JKAN B XSAKT SLBS OBX IAFVI AZS AJ DZXFVTXX BVW XLT IAS XANT SKTNTVWAZX WTBCX. HAZCW GAZ HBCC SLBS B "JFVBC IAAW DZG"?

Clue:
D = B

86

OX QKM UZMX ROMEAHWIWR XLKX BAKL AT SOSYW TKNW QKM NKIIOWR KBR LKR K QOTW BKNWR UAKB. MLAZYR MLW SW CBAQB KM XLW TOIMX “UAKB AT KIC”?

Clue:
C = K

87

T JZWPL WS TFJBOD DQAD WF T DLBIQTO IWHHQAABB SWZHBC AW CBABZHQFB MNW DNWPOC KB TCHQAABC AW NBTUBF. ANBX TZB ZBSBZZBC AW QF ZBOQJQWPD IQZIOBD TD “ANB DWPO-BZ LTFBO”.

Clue:
A = T

88

G WGLLRAU SNFZQA MGU G XNK GKU G UGFEMPAL. PMA XNK SNKXPGKPQT ZAXPALAU PMA UGFEMPAL GKU VLNFEMP MAL PN PAGLX. INFQU PMGP VA SNKXRUALAU G “YGWRQT SLT-XRX”.

Clue:
E = G

89

J OYGTFJFYL FLQOMYK TMPFQK JOK QKQBMQU TMBLQYT QO` QMT SQLTM YKQMQBO, HPM KQTMLQHPMYK MCYR JM OB UBTM. GBPVK MCQT HY JO YDJRFVY BS "SLYY-KPRH BS MCY FLYTT"?

Clue:
C = H

90

MGCTPL I BCTZTPIH KCTIH IP ICKTDK XITPKOM I XACKCITK AJ KSO IBBGDOM IPM SGPL TK AGKDTMO KSO BAGCK CAAZ. KSO XCTDAPOC OUBHITZOM “T’QO VOOP JCIZOM”.

Clue:
T = I

91

FP F YWNG PWRG HLTGMBP QWXNGB F VEBBD TM F XQWPGU PFDTMA DWE XFM'U XWRG WEU EMUTQ DWE EUUGL F HEMMD ZETO WL LIDRG. F HGS RTMEUGP QFUGL UIGD IGFLB ITR XLD WEU "WI-OEM UIG BWWL".

Clue:
H = F

92

EXUOSNQVC TQRGDYUEXF PSYP PQR OQQFW KYC EQP TSYCUEO YKYW PSX CIBUVVXDC PSYP KXVX RXEYTUEO PSX OYVFXEC QE PSX NDQTJ KSXVX PSXW YDD DULXF. PQR YOVXXF PQ ZQUE UE. PSX EXUOSNQVC CYUF “OQQFW PQQ CSQQC”.

Clue:
W = Y

93

IGJAS SDOX RXJAXDC UJEBOQ RMHD BRRKDR NBXU UBR LMNDAR MT IMOIDOXAJXBMO. UD VDIJHD MVGBEBMKR, CJYDC JOC IMHJ-GBSD. RUMKGC UBR JGXDA DQM VD ADOJHDC "RXKLMA HJO"?

Clue:
E = V

94

TP T QAIL PARBVTOFVP T PKANAOF VTOFW DAD IAJF TVW PAO UAMF LARVW PUFZ AVIZ UTW AVF QAIL MFQ DFPKFFV PUFO KUHXU PUFZ DAPU RNFW. KARIW ZAR XTII PUTP "IAJF, UAMF TVW NUTBF-T-PFF"?

Clue:
P = T

95

LT MPJJLFWWT, UFL KLCV TPGWN ALWC SMXWTN PTN ALWC SMLW FWTU UXREO LX UXWPURTD. PU UMW BRXVU MLQVW UMW LFTWX PVOWN "FML'V UMWXW?" UMW KLCV PTVFWXWN "ALWC". UMW GPT RTVRNW UMW MLQVW CWJJWN LQU "SMXWTN LX SMLW".

Clue:
S = P

96

VYJ NCUZCFJJE GTODGTG VJ LCPT C UDZLV JU VLT VJYU ZJDUZ HFJB JUT VCPTFU VJ CUJVLTF TUQJXDUZ VLT HDUT YDUT CUG ERDFDVE. D ZKTEE XJK OJKIG ECX VLTX YTFT "WCF LJRRDUZ".

Clue:
O = C

97

EQWTW SMO M LWTU CAEWIICZWAE IMJU SQD OECEGQWJ EDZWEQWT LWTU VWMYECNYI OSWMEWTO, VYE OQW DVPWGEWJ ED RWDRIW GDAOEMAEIU GMIICAZ QWT M "HACE-SCE".

Clue:
M = A

98

RF BRIWYFIRF, QUJ WUJJIJ IQVQJ, QBY LJF EVF XYE MYKJFYE, LE MYDZV VFZ LE KYSYFJ. QUJ KYQJEI IVRZ QUJN ZRZF'Q WVEJ LDWU XYE MYDZV TDQ BJEJ GEY KYSYFJ.

Clue:
K = V

99

K GPWTMEKC CKWTM REW LNYQTY UPNVM RTVV APWT KUDNV PCT VECTYA. RST KNMETCGT'A YTKGREPC UKA KVUKZA "PS QTTBT". UPNVM SEA YPNRECT LT GKVVTM K "QTTBT LNYQTY"?

Clue:
Q = G

100

K FKRNFKOO HCUBDNOENI XKJNE NIXDN OHIE VKE K INLCUKUDHX BHI FNDXA UVN FNRU DX UVN RLHIU. VN MKR KFON UH TKUTV JHIN FKOOR VDU UH UVN HCUBDNOE UVKX KXWHXN NORN. VN FNTKJN GXHMX KR "OHIE HB UVN BODNR".

Clue:
G = K

ANSWER KEY

ANSWER KEY

1

IF A FRUSTRATED WOODSMAN THREW HIS HATCHET INTO A WOODCHOPPING MACHINE, WOULD YOU SAY HE HAD AN AXE TO GRIND?

2

A FARMER AND HIS WIFE DECIDED TO HAVE LAMB CHOPS FOR DINNER. AFTER VIEWING BOTH THE MALE AND FEMALE LAMBS, THEY DECIDED THE FEMALE LOOKED MORE TENDER. TO WHICH THE MALE EXCLAIMED "BETTER EWE THAN ME".

ANSWER KEY

3

A YOUNG COUPLE IN LOVE TOOK A WALK ON AN OLD BOARDWALK IN A ROMANTIC OCEAN RESORT. AT THE END OF THE WALK THEY DISCOVERED THAT THEY BOTH HAD WOOD CHIPS IN THEIR FEET, BUT KISSED AND HUGGED ANYWAY. LOVE IS A MANY SPLINTERED THING.

4

A GROUP OF NEIGHBORS WHO WERE NOT INVITED TO A FRIENDS WEDDING, CRASHED THE CEREMONY ANYWAY. WOULD THEY BE CALLED "MARRY POP-INS"?

5

A MAN NAMED CAESAR FOUND A NEW HERBAL TEA CALLED "TUS" (TEA USING SAGE). WHEN HE VISITED A FRIEND HE WAS SURPRISED THAT HIS FRIEND SERVED HIM THE SAME TEA. CAESAR EXCLAIMED "YOU TOO BREW TUS".

ANSWER KEY

6

A MAN SUFFERED FROM UNCONTROLLABLE BLADDER PROBLEMS, SUCH THAT HE COULDN'T DANCE AT A PARTY LEST HE WET HIS PANTS. HE WAS INTRODUCED TO DEPENDS. HE WORE THEM ONE DAY TO A PARTY AND IT WORKED. WOULD THAT BE HIS IN DEPENDS DANCE DAY?

7

IF A FUNERAL DIRECTOR PAINTS HIS VEHICLE YELLOW INSTEAD OF THE TRADITIONAL BLACK, WOULD THAT BE A HEARSE OF A DIFFERENT COLOR?

8

IF A CHEF SAUTEED AND SERVED A MEAL THAT NOBODY COULD DISCERN WHAT IT WAS MADE OF. WOULD THAT BE AN UNIDENTIFIED FRYING OBJECT?

ANSWER KEY

9

MANNY BELIEVED IN HEAVEN AND HELL, BUT WAS CONVINCED HE WAS GOING TO HELL AND WANTED TO BE AS CLOSE AS POSSIBLE. HE LEFT A REQUEST IN HIS WILL TO "BURY MANNY LOW".

10

WOULD A MANSERVANT WHO ATTENDS TO THE HARD OF HEARING BE CALLED "' A VALET OF DEAF"?

11

IF MRS MELLON'S PET COLLIE HAD A PUPPY, WOULD IT BE "A MELLON COLLIE BABY"?

12

IN A WAR BETWEEN NATIONS IT REALLY DOESNT MATTER WHO WAS RIGHT. WHAT MATTERS IS WHO IS LEFT.

ANSWER KEY

13

IN A FOUR ROUND GOLF TOURNAMENT, IF YOU BIRDIE THE FIRST HOLE IN THE FIRST ROUND, YOU GET A BYE IN THE NEXT TWO ROUNDS. IS THAT A" BYE BYE BIRDIE"?

14

CHEF AMERICAS PASCAL SHREDDED SOME CHEESE SO THIN THAT NOBODY IN THE RESTAURANT COULD EVEN TASTE IT. SO, THE PATRONS ALL SHOUTED " MAKE AMERICAS GRATE AGAIN"!

15

IN A SOUTHERN PLANTATION, IF THE OWNERS SET UP A BELL TOWER TO ALERT THEM WHEN A STORM APPROACHES, WOULD THAT BE A “GONG WITH THE WIND”?

16

IN A FANTASY FOREST, IF AN ELM, A PINE AND AN OAK PUT ON A SLAP STICK COMEDY ROUTINE, WOULD THAT BE CALLED “THE TREE STOOGES”?

ANSWER KEY

17

A MAN WAS TOLD BY HIS DOCTOR TO NEVER DRINK COFFEE. HE CITED A TECHNICALITY AND STARTED DRINKING LATTE, EXCLAIMING “BETTER LATTE THAN NEVER”.

18

A COMPULSIVE GAMBLER WAS PROHIBITED FROM PLACING ANY MORE WAGES AT THE CASINO. SO HE ENLISTED A FRIEND TO PLACE THE BETS FOR HIM. WOULD THAT BE CONSIDERED “AIDING AND ABETTING”?

19

A GROUP OF FRIENDS SIT AROUND ALL DAY DOING NOTHING, THINKING NOTHING AND SAYING NOTHING. ONE DAY A MAN STANDS UP ON A CHAIR AND PROCLAIMS “I AM THE LEAST INTERESTED PERSON OF ALL OF US”. WOULD HE BE CONSIDERED THE CHAIRMAN OF THE BORED?

ANSWER KEY

20

IF A BRITISH SURGEON AND A U.S. MEDIC PERFORMED SURGERY ON AN INJURED SOLDIER'S ELBOW, WOULD THAT BE CALLED "A JOINT OPERATION"?

21

AT NIAGRA FALLS, A WARNING BELL WAS SET UP TO ALERT AUTHORITIES IF SOMEBODY FELL OVER THE FALLS. IF THE BELL WENT OFF BY ACCIDENT, WOULD THAT BE A "FALLS ALARM"?

22

A YOUNG GIRL SET UP A STAND TO SELL CUPS OF CUSTARD. A POLICEMAN ASKED HER IF SHE HAD A PERMIT. WHEN SHE ANSWERED NO, HE SHUT HER DOWN. WOULD THAT BE "CUSTARD"S LAST STAND"?

ANSWER KEY

23

THE BEATLES DID SO MUCH TRAVELING THAT THEIR CLOTHES BECAME SOILED VERY QUICKLY, HOWEVER, THEY BECAME EXPERTS AT LAUNDERING WITH A POPULAR DETERGENT ALMOST DAILY. IS THAT WHY THEY ARE CALLED "THE FAB FOUR"?

24

A MAN NAMED JACK SET UP A WEB SITE WHERE ANY MEMBER COULD SWAP THEIR MERCHNDISE WITH ANY OTHER MEMBER NO MATTER THE NATURE OR VALUE. WOULD HE BE CALLED "A JACK OF ALL TRADES"?

25

IF A COUPLE WHO TRAVELED THE GLOBE HAD A CHILD BORN AT THE NORTH POLE AND ONE BORN AT THE SOUTH POLE, WOULD THE CHILDREN BE CONSIDERED "BI-POLAR"?

ANSWER KEY

26

IN AN UPDATED VERSION OF THE FAMOUS RACE BETWEEN A RABBIT AND A TORTOISE THE RABBIT ACTUALLY WINS, BUT ONLY BY A "HARE".

27

PROFESSOR TATE CREATED A GPS SYSTEM THAT ALWAYS TAKES YOU TO THE WRONG PLACE. HE CALLED IT THE TATE SYSTEM AND SOLD IT USING THE SLOGAN "HE WHO HAS A TATES IS LOST".

28

IF AN NFL OWNER ERECTED A STADIUM SO THAT NO MATTER WHERE YOUR SEAT WAS LOCATED, YOU HAD A PERFECT UNOBSTRUCTED VIEW OF THE GAME, COULD THE CONTEST BE CALLED A "FAN-TO-SEE FOOTBALL GAME"?

ANSWER KEY

29

IN A COASTAL BAY A GROUP OF MILITARY MEDICS WERE BEING INSTRUCTED AS TO HOW TO CARE FOR SWIMMERS SUFFERING FROM AN ALGAE BLOOM. COULD THIS BE CALLED "BAY-SICK TRAINING"?

30

A NUTRITIONIST ADVISED HIS CLIENTS TO DRINK TEA DURING THE FALL, SAYING THAT THIS WOULD BE THE BEST CLIMATE FOR TEA. ALL THE CLIENTS COMPLAINED THAT THEY MISSED THEIR TEA. WAS THE NUTRITIONIST USING "FALL-TEA LOGIC"?

31

A MAN NAMED BUD FRANKEN CREATED A BEER MUG THAT WAS SO UGLY THAT IT WAS FRIGHTENING TO EVERYONE WHO SAW IT. BUD CALLED IT HIS "FRANKEN-STEIN". HIS FRIENDS EXCLAIMED THAT THEY THOUGHT BUD WISER THAN THAT.

ANSWER KEY

32

A CURE FOR A NEWLY DIAGNOSED INFECTION INVOLED A NEEDLE INJECTION WHICH ALSO RESULTED IN A STARTLING NEUROLOGIC REACTION. COULD THIS BE CALLED "STICKER SHOCK"?

33

IF SUPERMAN'S HUMAN ALTER EGO IS NO LONGER CAPABLE OF TRANSFORMING INTO THE CAPED CRUSADER, WOULD HE BE RIDICULED AND CALLED "CLARK CAN'T"?

34

IF ALL THE HORSES ON A RANCH WERE FED THE HEALTHIEST EQUINE FOOD AVAILABLE, WOULD THAT BE CONSIDERED A "STABLE DIET"?

35

IF DONALD DUCK SUDDENLY BECAME DISORIENTED AND SUFFERED FROM DEMENTIA WOULD HE THEN BECOME "DAFFY DUCK"?

ANSWER KEY

36

IN THE HIGHLY SOPHISTICATED GARDEN OF E-DEN, IF ADAM WAS ABLE TO HACK INTO EVE'S PRIVATE I-PHONE, WOULD YOU SAY HE TOOK A "BYTE OF THE FORBIDDEN APPLE"?

37

IF YOU WERE ACCUSED OF TRIPPING SOMEBODY SO THAT THEY STUMBLED AND INJURED THE JOINT IN THE MIDDLE OF THEIR LEG, WOULD THAT BE CONSIDERED A "FELL-ON-KNEE"?

38

IN THE NCAA BASKETBALL CHAMPIONSHIPS, THE LEAGUE HELD A GOLF TOURNAMENT. ON THE LAST HOLE, A PLAYER HIT A GOLF BALL THAT FLEW IN THE DIRECTION OF ANOTHER GOLFER AND YELLED "FORE". COULD THAT BE CALLED "THE FINAL FORE"?

ANSWER KEY

39

WOULD A POLICE OFFICER WHO WOULD CONSTANTLY SNEAK OFF DURING LUNCH HOUR TO TAKE A NAP BE CALLED "AN UNDERCOVER COP"?

40

A COUPLE WERE VISITING THE ALAMO WHEN THEY GOT INTO AN ARGUMENT, THE WIFE FELL AND BROKE THE MIDDLE JOINT IN HER LEG AND THEY GOT DIVORCED. THE HUSBAND CALLS HIS MONTHLY PAYMENTS TO HIS EX-WIFE "ALAMO-KNEE".

41

JUAN DIAZ WAS OUT PLAYING GOLF WHEN AN ERRANT GOLF SHOT PUNCTURED HIS LEG. COULD THAT BE CALLED "A HOLE IN JUAN"?

ANSWER KEY

42

ON THE LAST HOLE OF THE MASTERS GOLF TOURNAMENT IN GEORGIA, THE LEADERS BALL WAS BLOWN OUT OF BOUNDS BY A STRONG BREEZE AND HE LOST THE TOURNAMENT. HE BLAMED HIS LOSS ON "AUGUSTA WIND".

43

A GROUP OF FRIENDS WHO MET FOR MANY YEARS IN A SPECIAL SUITE AT A FANCY HOTEL DISCONTINUED THE GATHERING DUE TO OLD AGE AND ILLNESS. AS ONE FRIEND SAID, PARTING IS SUCH "SUITE SORROW".

44

IN AN UNLIT BATHROOM A WOMAN MISTAKENLY BRUSHED HER TEETH WITH GLUE FROM A TIN TUBE THAT LOOKED LIKE TOOTHPASTE. SHE WAS UNABLE TO EAT FOR SEVERAL DAYS. SHOULD SHE BE ON A "GLUE-TIN FREE DIET"?

ANSWER KEY

45

IF THE BANK OF MOUNT OLIVE OPENED AN OFFICE IN A COMPETING BANK'S LENDING AREA, WOULD THAT BE CONSIDERED "EXTENDING AN OLIVE BRANCH"?

46

IN A BEAUTY PAGEANT THE JUDGES HAD TO CHOOSE THE WINNER AMONG THREE FINALISTS; MARY, TERRY AND CHERRY. IF THEY CHOSE THE LATTER, WOULD THAT BE CONSIDERED "CHERRY PICKING"?

47

AT A SURPRISE BIRTHDAY PARTY, INSTEAD OF SOMEBODY POPPING OUT OF A LARGE CAKE, A VOCALIST STOOD ON TOP AND SANG HAPPY BIRTHDAY. COULD THAT BE CONSIDERED "THE I-SING ON THE CAKE"?

ANSWER KEY

48

A BEAUTY CONTESTANT WAS HOPING THAT SHE WOULD BE CROWNED THE WINNER. BUT SHE CAME IN SECOND. ON THE WAY OFF THE STAGE SHE TRIPPED AND CRACKED A TOOTH. SHE GOT HER "CROWN" ANYWAY.

49

IF A CITRUS COUNTY NEWSPAPER PHONED CONSTANTLY TO ASSESS ITS CUSTOMERS SATISFACTION WITH THEIR PRODUCT. WOULD YOU SAY THAT WAS A CITRUS COUNTY "CHRONIC-CALL"?

50

A MAN BY THE NAME OF LEWIS SIFFER PLAYED THE PART OF AN ANGEL IN A CHRISTMAS PAGEANT. DURING THE PERFORMANCE, HE TRIPPED AND FELL. COULD HE BE CALLED "LEW SIFFER THE FALLEN ANGEL"?

ANSWER KEY

51

IF AMOS BRIAR AND COMPANY DEVELOPED A CREAM THAT WHEN APPLIED TO THE EYES ALLEVIATED ALMOST ALL EYE AILMENTS. SHOULD THEY MARKET THE PRODUCT UNDER THE SLOGAN "FAMOUS AMOS BRIAR'S EYES CREAM"?

52

A COUPLE INSULTED AND YELLED AT EACH OTHER OVER SOME TRIVIAL MATTER, BUT THEN LATER COULDN'T REMEMBER OR FIGURE OUT WHY THEY WERE ARGUING IN THE FIRST PLACE. TO THEM IT BECAME "A CROSS-WORDS PUZZLE".

53

AT A TRIAL, THE DEFENSE ATTORNEY WROTE A POEM PROCLAIMING HIS CLIENT'S INNOCENCE. THE JUDGE REPLIED, ALTHOUGH YOU CAN RHYME, HE HAS TO DO TIME, THERE IS NO BAIL, HE IS GOING TO JAIL. WOULD THIS BE "POETIC JUSTICE"?

ANSWER KEY

54

A MAN SAW AN AD TO BUY A TWO DOLLAR LOTTO TICKET FOR ONE DOLLAR. WHEN HE WENT TO THE STORE ON SUNDAY TO BUY THE TICKET, HE DISCOVERED THE SALE ENDED SATURDAY. WOULD YOU SAY HE WAS "A DAY LATE AND A DOLLAR SHORT"?

55

HUMORIST MARK TWAIN HAD AN ALTER EGO NAMED STARK TWAIN WHO ALWAYS LOOKED ON THE DARK, STARK SIDE OF LIFE. BASED ON MARK'S STYLE OF WRITING, THE CRITICS DURING HIS LIFE WERE PRETTY CERTAIN THAT "NEVER THE TWAIN SHALL MEET".

56

WHEN A LADY ASKED A MAN HOW HIS GOLF WAS GOING, HE REPLIED "LIKE CLINT EASTWOOD". SHE RESPONDED "IT MAKES YOUR DAY?" NO, HE SAID "IT'S THE GOOD, THE BAD AND THE UGLY".

ANSWER KEY

57

IF TWO CANDIDATES RUNNING FOR THE HIGHEST OFFICE IN THE LAND COMPETED IN A CONTEST TO SEE WHO COULD REMOVE A WORM FROM A FISHHOOK THE QUICKEST, WOULD THAT BE CONSIDERED A PRESIDENTIAL DE-BAIT?

58

A COUPLE MET ON AN ON-LINE DATING SERVICE. THEY SHARED FACEBOOK AND TWITTER, BUT NEVER MET IN PERSON, AND WERE MARRIED IN A VIRTUAL CEREMONY CALLED WED ON THE WEB. COULD YOU SAY THEY "E-LOPED"?

59

A FRUSTRATED CHICKEN FARMER WAS LOOKING TO SEE IF HIS HENS WOULD FINALLY LAY EGGS. THEY WERE BARREN FOR MONTHS. WHILE HE WAS WATCHING, SUDDENLY THEY DELIVERED. COULD HIS OBSERVATION BE CALLED "EGG-SIGHTING"?

ANSWER KEY

60

THE CAPTAIN OF THE NEW YORK STATEN ISLAND FERRY RECOUNTED TO THE PASSENGERS ALL OF THE MANY STRANGE HAPPENINGS THAT OCCURRED DURING HIS VOYAGES IN THE HARBOR. WOULD THAT BE CONSIDERED "FERRY-TALES"?

61

A YOUNG GIRL RECEIVED A CHARM BRACELET FROM AN ADMIRER IN HIGH SCHOOL AND ANOTHER CHARM BRACET FROM A COLLEGE BEAU. ULTIMATELY, SHE MARRIED HER PRINCE CHARMING. WOULD YOU SAY SHE LED A "CHARMED LIFE"?

62

IF TWITTER EXISTED IN ANCIENT GREECE, WOULD THE MESSAGE SENT EXCLAIMING THE DISCOVERY OF THE FORMULA FOR THE AREA OF A CIRCLE BE CALLED A "TWEETY-PI"?

ANSWER KEY

63

IN THE DAYS OF THE ROMAN COLOSSEUM, A WOMAN HAD THE FIRST TRANSGENDER OPERATION AND BECAME A GLADIATOR. DURING A BATTLE, THE OPPONENT SAID YOU FIGHT LIKE A FEMALE. THE RESPONSE WAS "BEEN-HER".

64

WHEN THE MAN BEHIND THE PLATE IN A BASEBALL GAME REACTS ANGRILY TO THE BATTER'S CONSTANT OBJECTIONS TO HIS CALLS. WOULD YOU CALL THAT "UMP-IRE"?

65

WHILE ON A CLIMBING EXPEDITION IN THE ABOO MOUNTAINS IN INDIA, ONE MOUNTAINEER ASKED THE OTHER, "WOULD THE HIGHEST POINT IN THIS RANGE BE CALLED PEAK-ABOO"?

ANSWER KEY

66

WHEN A COUPLE WHO HAD BEEN MARRIED FIFTY YEARS HAD THEIR WEDDING RINGS STOLEN, THE HUSBAND BOUGHT NEW RINGS FOR ONE PENNY EACH. WHEN HIS WIFE DISCOVERED THE COST SHE EXCLAIMED "YOU ARE TWO-CENT-A-MENTAL".

67

A SLEEZY SALESMAN SOLD GOODS TO UNSUSPECTING CUSTOMERS THAT LATER TURNED OUT TO BE OBNOXIOUS AND DISGUSTING PRODUCTS. HE MADE A LOT OF MONEY IN THE PROCESS. WOULD THAT BE CONSIDERED "GROSS" PROFIT"?

68

THE PATRONS OF A GERMAN RESTAURANT PRAISED THE OWNER FOR THE QUALITY OF THE FOOD ON THE MENU, BUT SUGGESTED HE DO MORE ADVERTISING TO INCREASE THE VOLUME. HE COMPLIED WITH THE SLOGAN "OUR BRATS ARE THE WURST".

ANSWER KEY

69

A YOUNG GIRL NAMED MARY, WHO WAS AFRAID OF THE DARK, WAS GIVEN A SMALL ILLUMINATED DEVICE TO CALM HER FEARS AT NIGHT. MIGHT YOU SAY “MARY HAD A LITTLE LAMP”?

70

A COMEDIAN FELL AND INJURED HIS LEG WHICH CAUSED HIM TO WALK WITH A LIMP. HE RECOUNTED THE INCIDENT TO HIS AUDIENCE IN THE FORM OF A HUMOROUS STORY. MIGHT THAT BE CONSIDERED A “LAME JOKE”?

71

BOYCE CURLEY WAS INVITED TO A HALLOWEEN COSTUME PARTY. HOWEVER, HE DID NOT LIKE WEARING FAKE OUTFITS, SO HE WENT AS HIMSELF. I GUESS “BOYCE WILL BE BOYCE”.

ANSWER KEY

72

WHEN BARRY MULLIGAN, THE PUBLISHER OF A MAJOR SYNDICATED NEWSPAPER HIT A BAD SHOT OFF THE FIRST TEE IN A LOCAL GOLF TOURNAMENT, WOULD HE DARE SAY "DO I GET A MULLIGAN?"

73

A CHEF DECIDED TO BAKE A BATCH OF BARLEY LOAVES. BUT HE USED SO LITTLE FLOUR IN THE RECIPE, THE BREAD TURNED OUT TO BE EXTREMELY SMALL. THE PATRONS OF THE RESTAURANT SCREAMED "THESE ARE BARELY LOAVES".

74

AN ELDERLY MAGICIAN NAMED GERRY WAS ADMITTED TO A HOME FOR THE AGED. HOWEVER HE CONTINUED TO PERFORM FOR THE OTHER PATIENTS. THEY REFERRED TO HIS PERFORMANCE AS "GERRY–AT—TRICKS".

ANSWER KEY

75

BARRY GOLD HAD A BAD TENDENCY TO INTERFERE WITH EVERYBODY ELSE'S BUSINESS. HIS FRIENDS CREATED AND PRESENTED TO HIM A SPECIAL TROPHY THEY CALLED "A GOLD MEDDLE".

76

TOM MOORE, A VERY ROMANTIC GENTLEMAN HAS BEEN MARRIED TEN TIMES AND IS ENGAGED TO ANOTHER LOVELY LADY WHO WILL BECOME HIS ELEVENTH BRIDE. HIS FRIENDS REFER TO HIM AS THE "MOORE THE MARRIER".

77

IN AFRICA A HERD OF GNUS GRAZED ACROSS THE VAST PLAINS. THEN A SMALL GROUP BROKE AWAY AND FORMED THEIR OWN HERD. WOULD THIS BE CONSIDERED "BREAKING GNUS"?

ANSWER KEY

78

A GROUP OF ARCHAEOLOGISTS, WHILE EXPLORING THE JUNGLES OF AFRICA DISCOVERED THE REMAINS OF AN EXTINCT TRIBE THAT HAD EQUINE FEATURES. WOULD THAT BE TERMED A "HORSE RACE"?

79

MANY ARTISTS TRIED TO PAINT THE LIKENESS OF A BEAUTIFUL GIRL BY THE NAME OF DEE, A NICKNAME FOR SANDY, BUT TO NO AVAIL. FINALLY SOMEBODY WAS SUCCESSFUL. THE OTHER ARTISTS PONDERED "HOW'D HE DO DEE"?

80

IN A FLOCK OF SHEEP, IF A FEMALE, WHO HAD A COLD, SNEEZED. WOULD IT BE PROPER FOR THE MALE SHEEP TO SAY "GOD BLESS EWE"?

ANSWER KEY

81

A GROUP OF NEIGHBORING CHURCHES CONDUCTED A POLL TO DETERMINE WHICH OF THEIR RELIGIOUS LEADERS WAS CONSIDERED THE BEST. WOULD THE WINNER BE CONSIDERED "THE PRIME MINISTER"?

82

ON A COLD WINTER'S DAY, A GROUP OF AVID TEN-PIN ADVOCATES SET UP AN ALLEY ON A FROZEN POND. COULD THAT BE CALLED "A BOWL OF CHILLY"?

83

THIS YEAR ON DECEMBER TWENTY FIFTH THE ARMY HAD TO HAUL BACK TO SHORE A BALLISTIC MISSILE THAT MISFIRED. IT WILL BE FOREVER KNOWN AS THE "MISSILE-TOWED CHRISTMAS".

ANSWER KEY

84

JOE WITTS AND HIS BROTHER JOHN WITTS DISAGREED ON ALMOST EVERYTHING, AND AS A RESULT THEY WERE CONSTANTLY FIGHTING EACH OTHER. WOULD THAT BE CONSIDERED A "BATTLE OF THE WITTS"?

85

A WOMAN PURCHASED THE LAST ITEMS ON SALE FROM A STORE THAT WAS GOING OUT OF BUSINESS AND SHE GOT SOME TREMENDOUS DEALS. COULD YOU CALL THAT A "FINAL GOOD BUY"?

86

IT WAS JUST DISCOVERED THAT NOAH OF BIBLE FAME WAS MARRIED AND HAD A WIFE NAMED JOAN. SHOULD SHE BE KNOWN AS THE FIRST "JOAN OF ARK"?

ANSWER KEY

87

A GROUP OF ANGELS SITS ON A SPECIAL COMMITTEE FORMED TO DETERMINE WHO SHOULD BE ADMITTED TO HEAVEN. THEY ARE REFERRED TO IN RELIGIOUS CIRCLES AS "THE SOUL-ER PANEL".

88

A MARRIED COUPLE HAD A SON AND A DAUGHTER. THE SON CONSTANTLY PESTERED THE DAUGHTER AND BROUGHT HER TO TEARS. WOULD THAT BE CONSIDERED A "FAMILY CRY-SIS".

89

A NEWSPAPER PRINTED STUPID AND IDIOTIC STORIES IN ITS FIRST EDITION, BUT DISTRIBUTED THEM AT NO COST. WOULD THIS BE AN EXAMPLE OF "FREE-DUMB OF THE PRESS"?

ANSWER KEY

90

DURING A CRIMINAL TRIAL AN ARTIST PAINTED A PORTRAIT OF THE ACCUSED AND HUNG IT OUTSIDE THE COURT ROOM. THE PRISONER EXCLAIMED "I'VE BEEN FRAMED".

91

AS A JOKE SOME FRIENDS LOCKED A BUDDY IN A CLOSET SAYING YOU CAN'T COME OUT UNTIL YOU UTTER A FUNNY QUIP OR RHYME. A FEW MINUTES LATER THEY HEARD HIM CRY OUT "OH-PUN THE DOOR".

92

NEIGHBORS COMPLAINED THAT TOM GOODY WAS NOT CHASING AWAY THE SQUIRRELS THAT WERE MENACING THE GARDENS ON THE BLOCK WHERE THEY ALL LIVED. TOM AGREED TO JOIN IN. THE NEIGHBORS SAID "GOODY TOO SHOOS".

ANSWER KEY

93

CLARK KENT STARTED HAVING SOME ISSUES WITH HIS POWERS OF CONCENTRATION. HE BECAME OBLIVIOUS, DAZED AND COMA-LIKE. SHOULD HIS ALTER EGO BE RENAMED "STUPOR MAN"?

94

AT A GOLF TOURNAMENT A TWOSOME NAMED BOB LOVE AND TOM HOPE FOUND THEY ONLY HAD ONE GOLF PEG BETWEEN THEM WHICH THEY BOTH USED. WOULD YOU CALL THAT “LOVE, HOPE AND SHARE-A-TEE”?

95

ON HALLOWEEN, TWO BOYS, NAMED JOEY PHREND AND JOEY PHOE WENT TRICK OR TREATING. AT THE FIRST HOUSE THE OWNER ASKED “WHO’S THERE?” THE BOYS ANSWERED “JOEY”. THE MAN INSIDE THE HOUSE YELLED OUT “PHREND OR PHOE”.

ANSWER KEY

96

TWO KANGAROOS DECIDED TO HAVE A NIGHT ON THE TOWN GOING FROM ONE TAVERN TO ANOTHER ENJOYING THE FINE WINE AND SPIRITS. I GUESS YOU COULD SAY THEY WERE "BAR HOPPING".

97

THERE WAS A VERY INTELLIGENT LADY WHO STITCHED TOGETHER VERY BEAUTIFUL SWEATERS, BUT SHE OBJECTED TO PEOPLE CONSTANTLY CALLING HER A "KNIT-WIT".

98

IN WISCONSIN, THE CHEESE STATE, TWO MEN RAN FOR GOVERNOR, MR GOUDA AND MR VOLONE. THE VOTERS SAID THEY DIDN'T CARE MUCH FOR GOUDA BUT WERE PRO VOLONE.

ANSWER KEY

99

A COMEDIAN NAMED TIM BURGER WOULD TELL SOME AWFUL ONE LINERS. THE AUDIENCE'S REACTION WAS ALWAYS "OH GEEZE". WOULD HIS ROUTINE BE CALLED A "GEEZE BURGER"?

100

A BASEBALL OUTFIELDER NAMED ERNIE LORD HAD A REPUTATION FOR BEING THE BEST IN THE SPORT. HE WAS ABLE TO CATCH MORE BALLS HIT TO THE OUTFIELD THAN ANYONE ELSE. HE BECAME KNOWN AS "LORD OF THE FLIES".

Made in the USA
Middletown, DE
09 April 2017